SCIENCE FUSion

Interactive Student Edition

Printed in the U.S.A.

ISBN 978-0-547-36794-1

19 0877 19 18

4500715091 ABCDE

HOUGHTON MIFFLIN HARCOURT

Contents

Our Senses

touch

smell

hear

see

taste

Name _____

see

hear

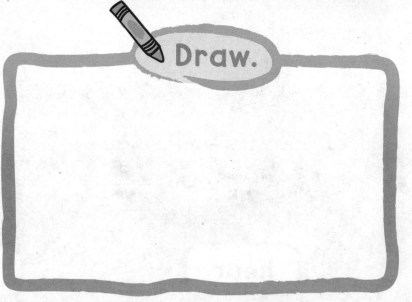

Draw.

Your senses help you learn.
You see things with your eyes.
You hear sounds with your ears.

▶ Draw something you see.

Name _____

touch

smell

taste

You touch things with your hands and skin.

You smell things with your nose.

You taste foods with your mouth.

Sum It Up!

● Circle the child hearing something. ▲ Circle the child seeing something. ■ Circle the child tasting something.

Science Skills

observe

compare

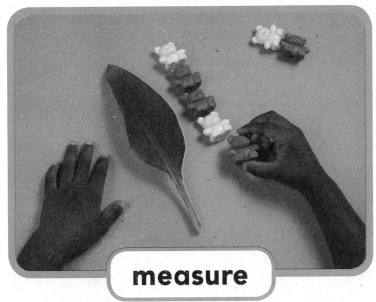

measure

big | **small**

sort

© Houghton Mifflin Harcourt Publishing Company   (tl) ©Blend Images/Alamy

Name _____

observe

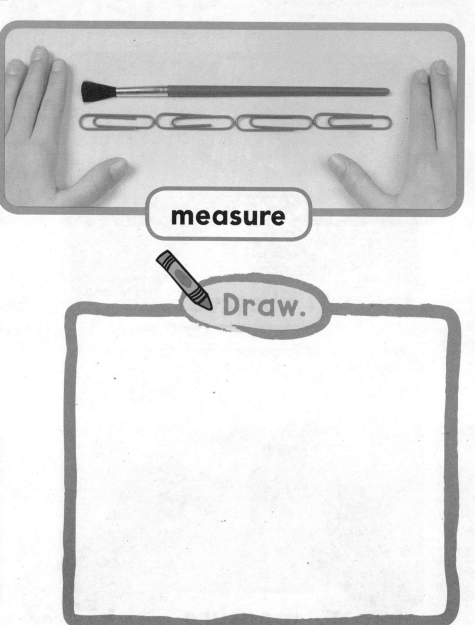

measure

Draw.

We ask questions to learn.
We observe to find answers.
We measure to find answers.

▶ Observe your hand. Draw what you observe.

Name _____

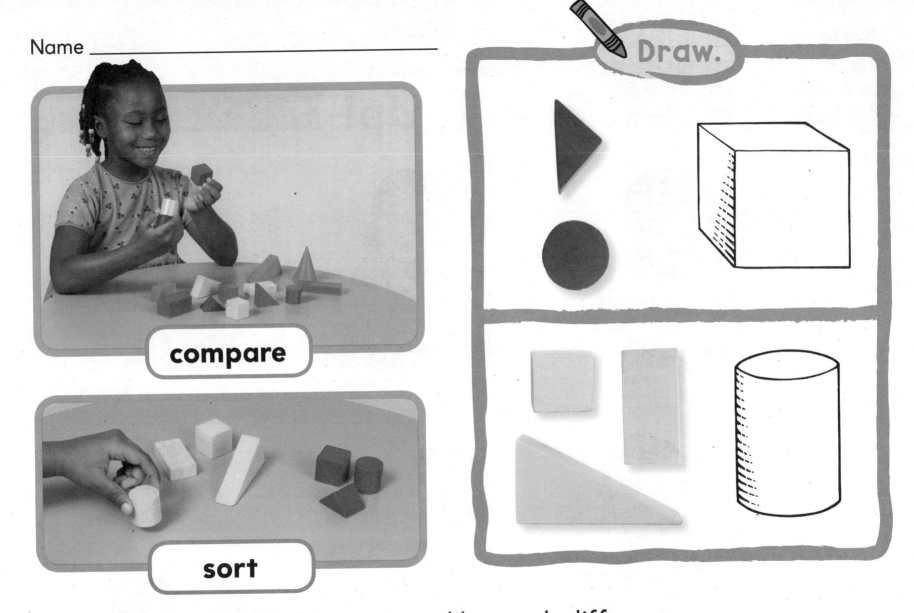

compare

sort

Draw.

We compare how things are alike and different.
We sort things that are alike into groups.

© Houghton Mifflin Harcourt Publishing Company

▶ Color each block to match its group.

Sum It Up!

● Circle the child measuring something.
▲ Circle the child sorting things.

Science Tools

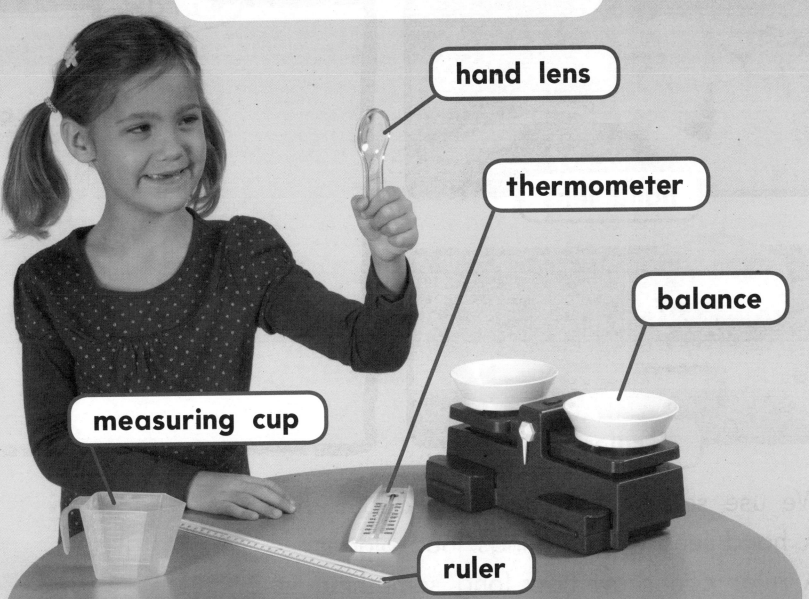

hand lens

thermometer

balance

measuring cup

ruler

Name _____

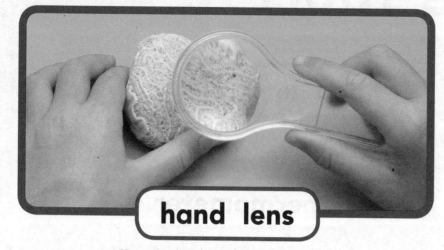

hand lens

ruler

Draw.

We use science tools to learn about things.
A hand lens makes things look bigger.
A ruler can show how long something is.

▶ Draw something you can measure with a ruler.

Name _____

balance

thermometer

measuring cup

A balance shows which thing is heavier.

A thermometer shows how warm it is.

A measuring cup shows how much water.

► Circle the thermometer.

Sum It Up!

● Circle the ruler.   Circle the measuring cup.
■ Circle the hand lens.

Living and Nonliving

living things

nonliving things

Name _____

water

food

place to live

Living things need food and water.
They also need a place to live.
Do nonliving things need these?

▶ Circle the living thing getting food.

new plant

ducks

Draw.

Plants can make more plants.
Animals can have young.
Can nonliving things do this?

▶ Draw a living thing getting water.

Sum It Up!

● Circle the living thing.   Circle the nonliving thing.

Real and Pretend

real

pretend

Name _____

real

pretend

Draw.

Pretend animals can do things real animals can not do.

▶ Draw a real animal.

Name _____

pretend

Draw.

Pretend plants can do things real plants can not do.

▶ Draw a real plant.

Name _____

Sum It Up!

  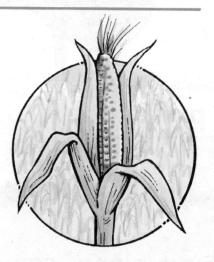

● Circle the real thing.
▲ Circle the pretend thing.

Many Animals

fur

feathers

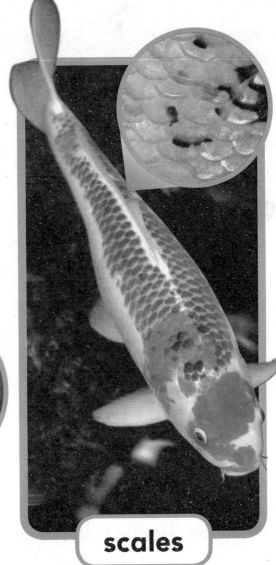

scales

Name _____

blue jay

ladybug

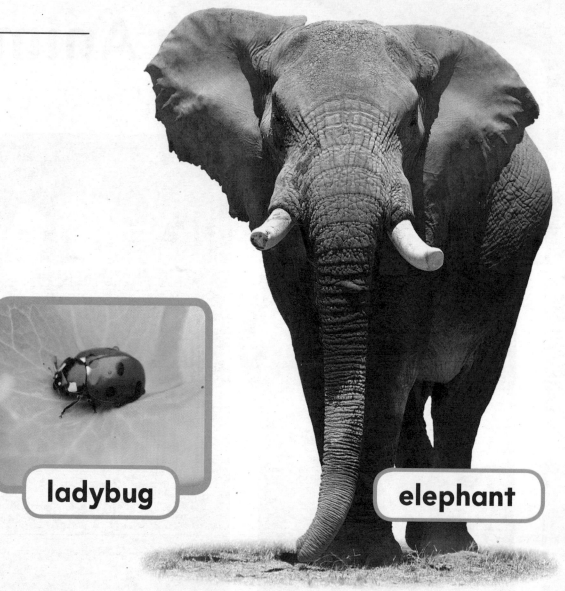

elephant

Animals have different shapes and sizes.
Some animals have bright colors.

▶ Circle the blue animal. Draw a line under the smallest animal.

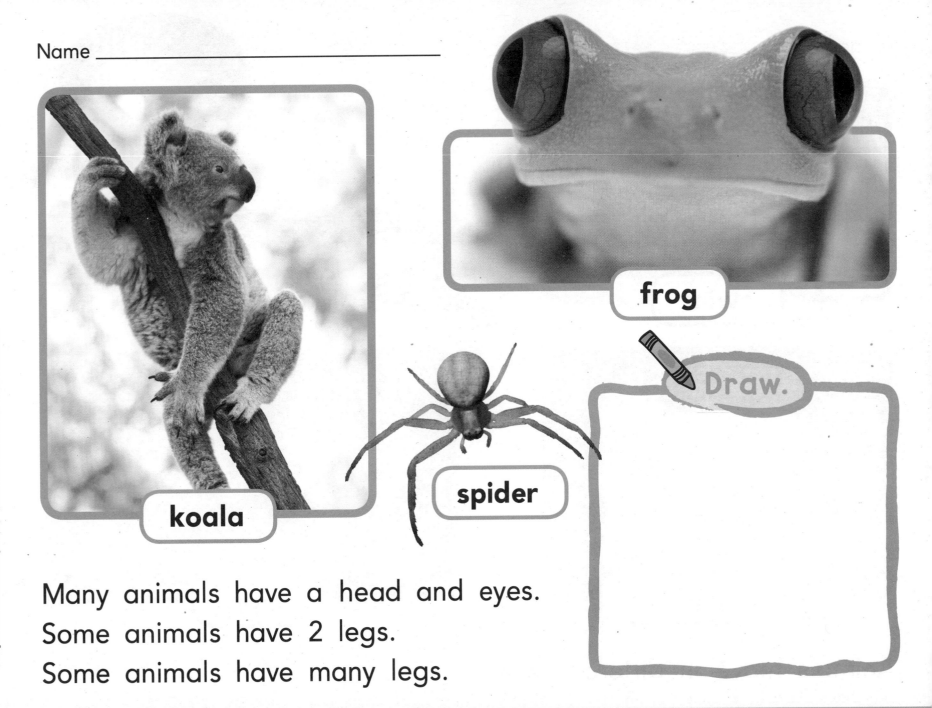

Name _____

koala

frog

spider

Draw.

Many animals have a head and eyes.
Some animals have 2 legs.
Some animals have many legs.

▶ Draw the head and eyes of an animal.

Name _____

swim

crawl

walk and run

hop

Animals move in different ways.

▶ Circle the animal that crawls.

Name _____

fly

Which animal hops?
Which animal swims?
Which animal walks and runs?

Draw.

▶ Draw an animal that flies.

Sum It Up!

● Circle the animal that has fur. ▲ Circle the animal that swims. ■ Circle the animal that flies.

What Animals Need

food

air

water

shelter

Name _____

shelter

food

water

Animals need food, water, and air — just like you.
Animals need shelter — just like you.

▶ Circle the bear getting food.

Name _____

food

Draw.

Pets need people to give them food, water, and shelter.

▶ Draw a pet getting food and water.

Sum It Up!

Circle the things the squirrel needs.

Animals Grow and Change

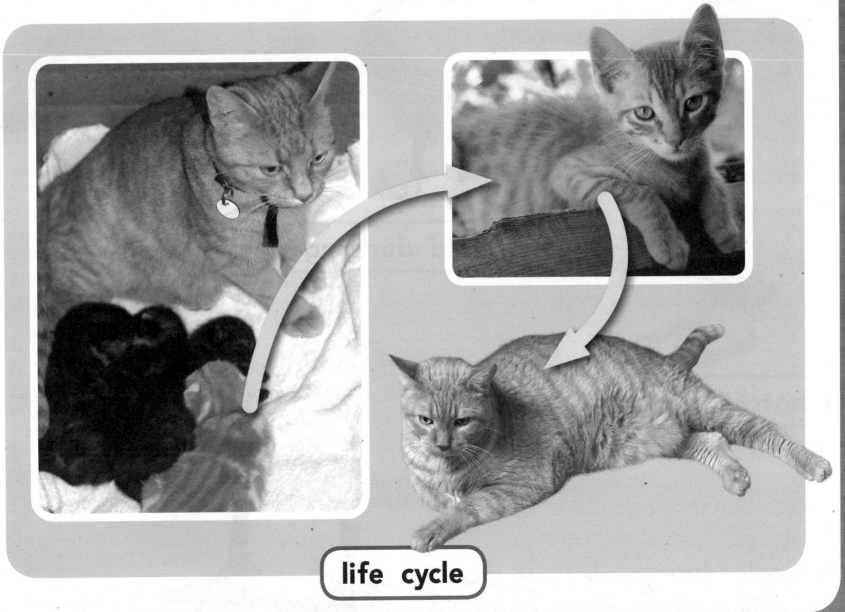

life cycle

Name _____

month-old duckling

hatchling duck

adult duck

Animals change as they grow.

▶ Circle the hatchling duck.

Name _____

frog eggs

tadpole with 2 legs

adult frog

tadpole with 4 legs

▶ Circle the adult frog.

© Houghton Mifflin Harcourt Publishing Company   (tl) ©Premierlight/Alamy; (tr) ©Robert Clay/Alamy; (bl) ©Derek Croucher/Alamy; (br) ©Harry Rogers/Photo Researchers, Inc.

Sum It Up!

●

▲

● Circle the adult dog.
  Circle the newborn horse.

Many Plants

grass

tree

shrub

trees

Plants can be trees, grasses, and shrubs.
There are many kinds of trees.

Draw.

▶ Draw a tree.

Name _____

grasses

shrubs

There are many kinds of grasses.
There are many kinds of shrubs.

▶ Circle the tall grass.

Sum It Up!

● Circle the tree.   Circle the shrub.

What Plants Need

light

air

soil

space to grow

water

© Houghton Mifflin Harcourt Publishing Company ©Getty Images

Name _____

water

no water

Draw.

Plants need air, light, and water to live.

▶ Draw a plant getting water.

Name _____

Draw.

space to grow

soil

Plants need soil.
Plants need space to grow.

▶ Most plants get the light they need from the sun. Draw the sun.

Sum It Up!

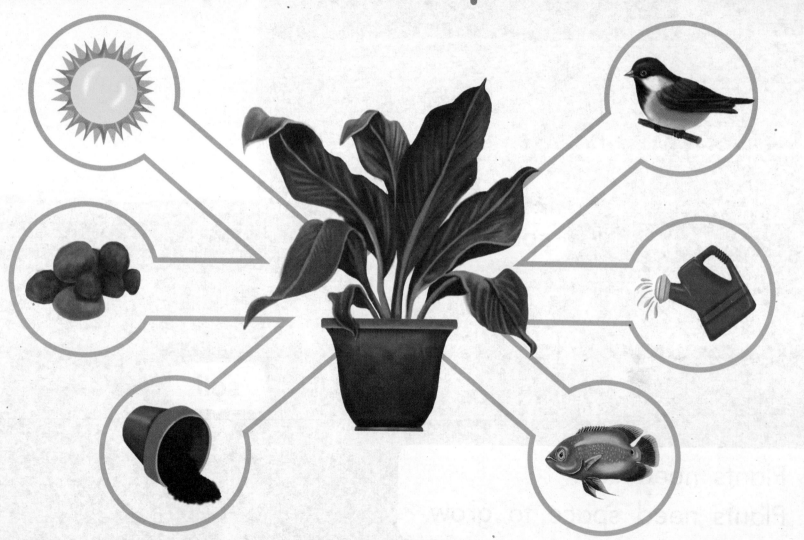

Draw a line to each thing the plant needs.

Plant Parts

leaf

flower

fruit

roots

stem

seeds

Name _____

leaves

Draw.

flowers

Plants are made up of parts.
There are many kinds of leaves and flowers.

▶Draw a leaf in the top box. Draw a flower in the bottom box.

Name _____

seeds

© Houghton Mifflin Harcourt Publishing Company   (t) ©Martin Bennett/Alamy; (c) ©Ryan Mcvay/Getty Images; (b) ©foodfolio/Alamy

Draw.

Fruit grows from the flowers of some plants.
Seeds grow in the fruit.

▶ Draw a fruit.

Name _____

Sum It Up!

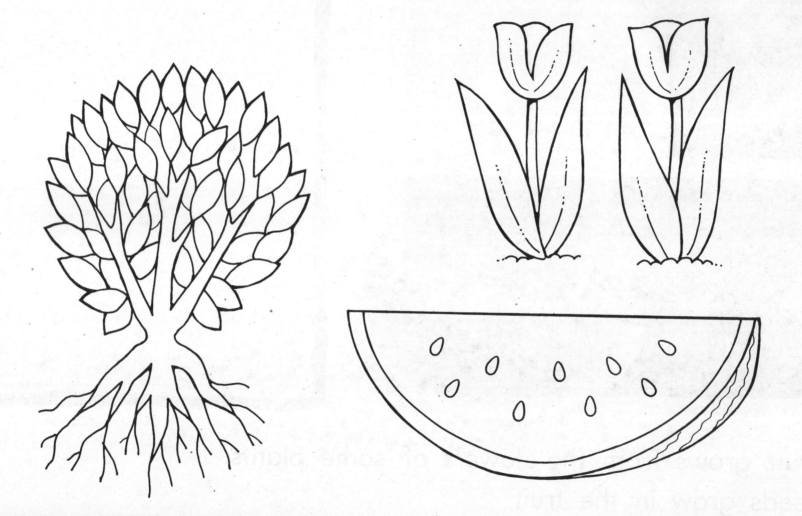

Color the roots brown. Color the stems and leaves green.
Color the flowers yellow. Color the fruit red. Color the seeds black.

Plants Grow and Change

seed

flower

sprout

seedling

adult plant

seed

sprout

seedling

A plant has a life cycle.
A plant changes as it grows.

► Circle the seed.

Name _____

Draw.

young tree

adult tree

► Draw a young tree.

© Houghton Mifflin Harcourt Publishing Company   ©RTimages/Alamy

Name _____

Sum It Up!

Circle the sprout. Draw a line under the adult tree.

Homes for Living Things

habitat

Name _____

pond

ocean

Houghton Mifflin Harcourt Publishing Company (l) ©First Light/Alamy; (l, inset) ©Natural Visions/Alamy; (r) ©Greg Wright/Alamy; (r, inset) ©Dave Porter/Alamy

Some animals and plants live in water habitats.

▶ Circle the ocean habitat.

Name _____

desert

rain forest

Some animals and plants live in land habitats.
The animals and plants get what they need from their habitats.

▶ Circle the desert habitat.

Sum It Up!

● Circle the pond habitat.
▲ Circle the rain forest habitat.

Animals and Plants Together

shelter

Name _____

shelter

food

Some animals use plants for shelter.
Many animals need plants for food.

▶ Circle the animals using a plant for shelter.

Name _____

squirrel

acorn

Draw.

Plants need animals.

Animals move seeds.

The seeds may grow to become new plants.

▶ Draw a new plant that may grow from
the acorn the squirrel is moving.

Sum It Up!

● Circle the animal using a plant for food.
▲ Circle the animal using a plant for shelter.
■ Circle the animal moving a seed.

© Houghton Mifflin Harcourt Publishing Company

Day Sky

sky

sun

clouds

© Houghton Mifflin Harcourt Publishing Company ©ImageClick, Inc./Alamy

morning

noon

afternoon

We see the sun in the sky during the day.

We also see clouds and other objects in the sky.

During the day, the sun seems to move across the sky.

▶ Circle the sun in each picture.

Name _____

far

near

Draw.

Objects near Earth look big.
Objects far from Earth look small.

© Houghton Mifflin Harcourt Publishing Company ©istop2/Alamy

▶ Draw the sky during the day.

Sum It Up!

● Circle the sun in the morning.
▲ Circle the sun in the middle of the day.
■ Circle the sun in the afternoon.

Night Sky

stars

moon

moon

Draw.

At night we may see stars in the sky.
On most nights we see the moon.

▶ Draw the moon.

Name _____

We may also see the moon during the day.

▶ Circle the moon.

Sum It Up!

● Draw the day sky. ▲ Draw the night sky.

Rocks

rocks

Name _____

different sizes

different shapes

Rocks are nonliving things.
Rocks can be different sizes, shapes, colors, and textures.

© Houghton Mifflin Harcourt Publishing Company   (l) ©imagebroker/Alamy; (square rock) ©The Natural History Museum/Alamy

▶ Circle the smallest rock.

Name _____

Draw.

| different colors | different textures |

Some rocks are smooth.
Some rocks are rough.

▶ Draw two rocks that are different colors.

Sum It Up!

Draw an X on each rock.

Water

water

Name _____

river

lake

ocean

Water covers most of Earth.
Water is found in rivers, lakes, and oceans.

▶ Draw an X on the river.

Name _____

pond

Draw.

Clean water is clear.
Is the water in this pond clean?

▶ Draw a fish you might see in this pond.

Sum It Up!

● ▲ ■ ★   Color the water blue.

Natural Resources

rock

water

soil

Name _____

carrots growing in soil

carrots

Soil is a natural resource.
Most plants need soil to grow.
Many plants are food for people.

▶ Circle the carrots being used for food.

Name _____

bridge

Draw.

Rocks are a natural resource.
We use rocks to make things.

Name _____

We drink water.

Water is a natural resource.
We need water to live.
We should use water carefully.

Turn off water after use.

Draw.

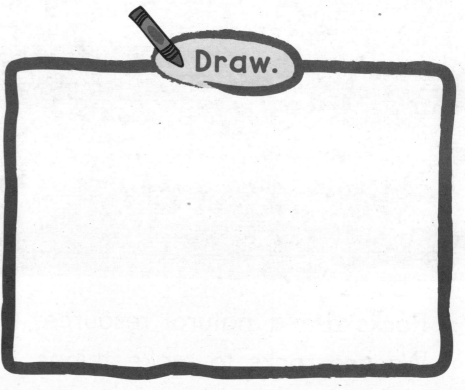

▶ Draw a way to use water carefully.

Name _____

recycle

reuse

We can care for natural resources.

We can recycle things.

We can reuse things.

► Circle something being reused.

Name _____

Sum It Up!

●

▲

■

● Circle the picture showing soil being used.
▲ Circle the picture showing water being used carefully.
■ Circle the picture showing something being reused.

© Houghton Mifflin Harcourt Publishing Company

Weather

sunny

snowy

rainy

cloudy

windy

cloudy weather

sunny weather

There are many kinds of weather.
Some days are cloudy.
Some days are sunny.

▶ Circle the cloudy day.

Name _____

Draw.

windy weather

Some days are windy.

▶ Draw a tree on a windy day.

Name _____

rainy weather

Draw.

Some days are rainy.

On a rainy day, we play inside.

► Draw something you like to do on a rainy day.

Name _____

snowy weather

Some days are snowy.
Snowy days are cold.

▶ Circle the children playing in the snowy weather.

Name _____

Sum It Up!

●

▲

■

● Circle the snowy weather. ▲ Circle the rainy weather.
■ Circle the sunny weather.

Measuring Weather

thermometer

windsock

Name _____

high temperature

low temperature

We use tools to measure weather.
A thermometer tells how hot or cold it is.

▶ Circle the thermometer that shows a low temperature.

Name _____

not windy

windy

Draw.

A windsock shows if it is windy.

▶ Draw a windsock on a windy day.

Name _____

Sum It Up!

●

▲

■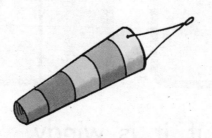

● ▲ ■ Circle the tool each child could use to measure the weather shown.

Seasons

spring

summer

winter

fall

spring

The seasons follow a pattern.
In spring, animals are born or hatched.
Warm weather helps plants grow.

► Circle the young animals.

Name _____

summer

Summer comes after spring.
In summer, plants grow bigger.
Young animals grow and learn.

▶ Circle the young deer doing what its mother is doing.

Name _____

fall

Fall comes after summer.
Leaves, nuts, and fruit fall from the trees.
Animals get ready for winter.

▶ Circle the animal getting ready for winter.

Name _____

winter

Draw.

Winter comes after fall.
Many trees lose all their leaves.
Some animals change in winter.

▶ Draw what winter is like where you live.

Name _____

Sum It Up!

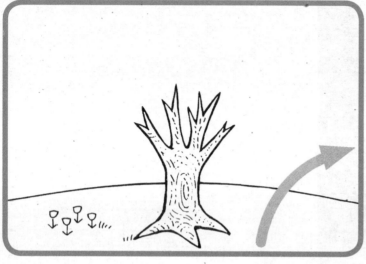 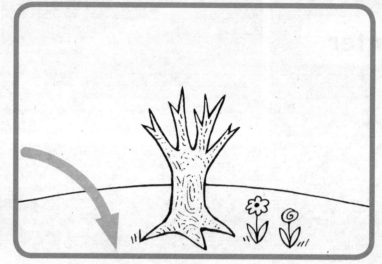

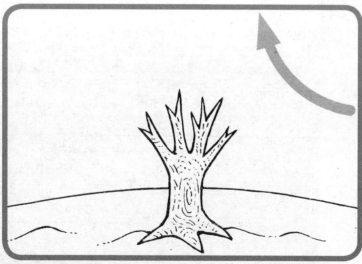 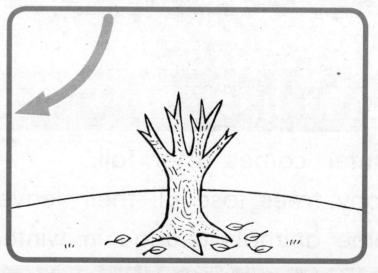

Show what the tree looks like in spring, summer, fall, and winter.

Matter

matter

Name _____

liquid

gas

solid

Matter is anything that takes up space.
Matter can be a liquid, a gas, or a solid.

© Houghton Mifflin Harcourt Publishing Company ©Getty Images

▶ Draw an X on the liquid.

Name _____

different sizes

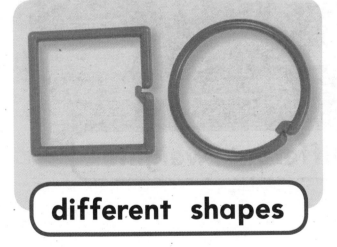

different shapes

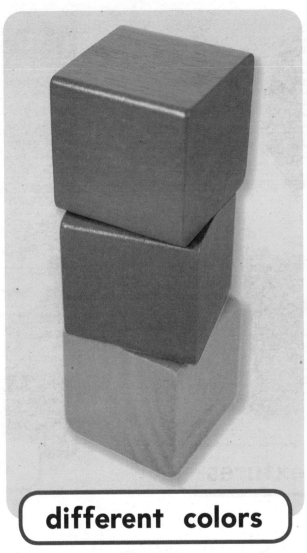

different colors

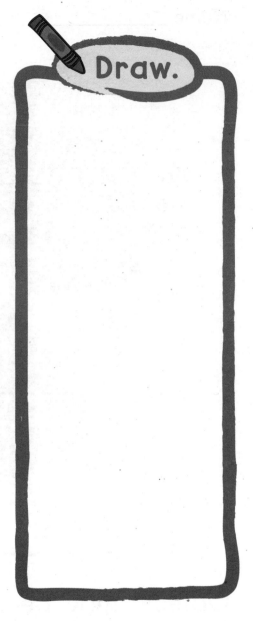

Draw.

Objects are different sizes, shapes, and colors.

▶ Draw an object you can tell about.

Name _____

different textures

different weights

Objects may be rough or smooth.
Objects may be heavy or light.

▶ Circle the object that is rough.

Name _____

different temperatures

Draw.

Things may be hot or cold.

Sum It Up!

●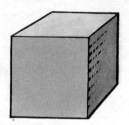

▲

■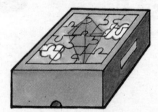

● Circle the object that is a different color.
▲ Circle the object that is a different size.
■ Circle the object that is a different shape.

Matter Can Change

change

Name _____

tear	smash

 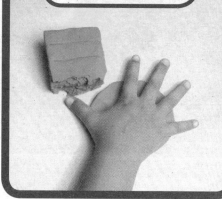

roll	bend

We can change clay.

Draw.

▶ Draw something you can make from clay.

Name _____

cut

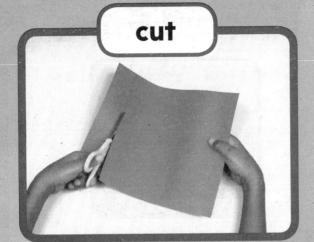

fold

crumple

We can change paper.

▶ Circle the paper being cut.

Sum It Up!

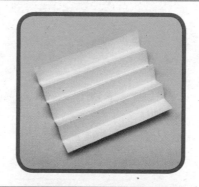

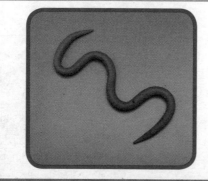

● Circle the paper that is cut. ▲ Circle the paper that is folded.
■ Circle the clay that is smashed.

Heating and Cooling Matter

heat

cool

Name _____

raw egg

heating

Draw.

cooked egg

Matter may change when it heats up.

▶ Draw a cooked egg.

Name _____

liquid

cooling

solid

When matter cools, it may change.
A liquid may become a solid.

▶ Circle the matter being cooled.

Sum It Up!

● Circle what happens when water is cooled.

▲ Circle what happens when pancake batter is heated.

Sound

sound

vibrate

soft

loud

Draw.

Things vibrate back and forth.
This makes a sound.
Sounds may be loud or soft.

▶ Draw something that makes a loud sound.

Name _____

low

high

Draw.

Sounds may be low or high.
What makes a very low sound?

© Houghton Mifflin Harcourt Publishing Company (l) ©Image Source/Getty Images

Sum It Up!

● Circle the person making a soft sound.
▲ Circle the person making a low sound.

Light

light

Name _____

sun

lamp

flashlight

Draw.

The sun gives off light.
Some things people make give off light.
What other things give off light?

▶ Draw something that gives off light.

Name _____

very little light

a lot of light

We need light to see things.

▶ Circle the room with more light.

Sum It Up!

Circle the things that give off light.

Heat

heat

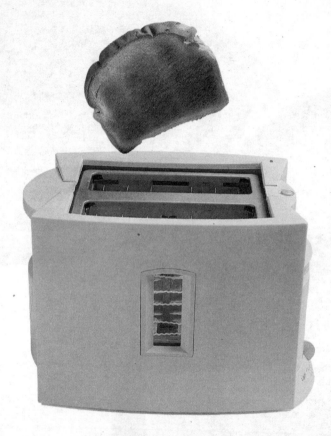

toaster

clothes dryer

Some things give off heat.

▶ Circle the thing that uses heat to toast bread.

Name _____

sun

candle

Draw.

Many things give off both heat and light.

▶ Draw something that gives off heat and light.

Sound, light, and heat are kinds of energy.
Energy can make things change.

▶ Circle the sources of sound, light, or heat energy.

Name _____

Sound energy helps you hear.
Light energy helps you see.
Heat energy keeps you warm.

▶ Circle the sources of sound, light, or heat energy.

Sum It Up!

● Circle the thing that gives off light.   ▲ Circle the thing that makes sound.   ■ Circle the thing that gives off heat.

Where Things Are

beside

above

below

behind

in front of

© Houghton Mifflin Harcourt Publishing Company

Name _____

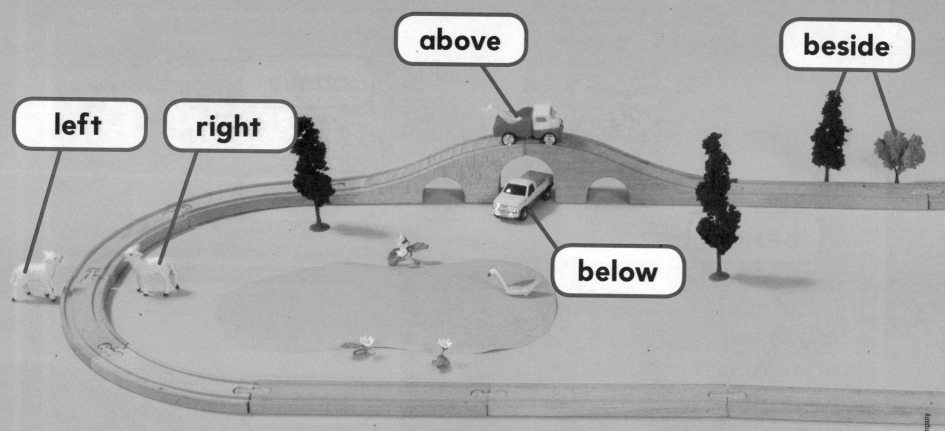

left right above beside below

You can use words to tell where things are.

► Circle the truck below the bridge.

Name _____

in

out

in front of

behind

Where are the ducks?

▶ Draw a ball with a tree behind it.

Name _____

Sum It Up!

Color the toy above the airplane yellow. Color the toy below the truck blue. Color the toy beside the ball green. Color the toy in front of the basket orange.

How Things Move

zigzag

round and round

straight

up and down

back and forth

straight

round and round

Things move in different ways.

▶ Color the arrows to show the direction things are moving.

Name _____

up and down

Things may change direction.

back and forth

zigzag

© Houghton Mifflin Harcourt Publishing Company (l) ©John Lawrence Photography/Alamy; (tr) ©SnowyWelsh/Alamy; (br) ©Getty Images

▶ Color the arrows to show the direction things are moving.

Name _____

fast

Sometimes things move fast.

▶ Draw an X on the animal that can move fast.

Name _____

 Draw.

slow

Sometimes things move slowly.

▶ Draw something that can move slowly.

© Houghton Mifflin Harcourt Publishing Company   (l) ©First Light/Alamy

Sum It Up!

  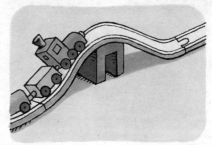

● Circle the train that goes straight. ▲ Circle the marble that goes round and round. ■ Circle the animal that moves slowly.

Changing How Things Move

push

pull

Name _____

push

pull

We can push and pull things.
We can change the direction things move.

▶ Circle the person pulling something.

Name _____

gravity

Gravity pulls things down unless something holds them up.

▶ Draw an arrow to show where the ball will go.

Unit 10 • Lesson 31 • How Can We Change the Way Things Move?

Sum It Up!

● Circle the person pushing.
▲ Circle the person pulling.

Magnets

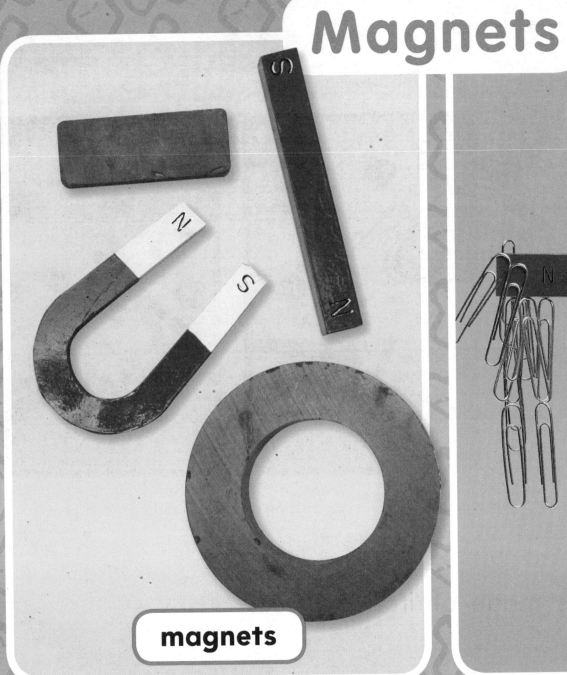

magnets

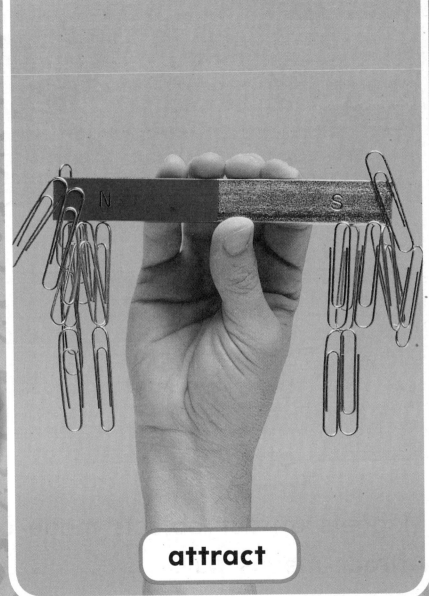

attract

Name _____

attract

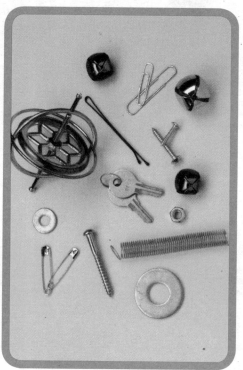

Magnets attract objects made of iron or steel.
Attract means pull.

▶ Circle the group of objects a magnet will attract.

Name _____

magnet

Draw.

Magnets can move some objects without touching them.

▶ Draw an arrow to show the direction the truck is moving.

Sum It Up!

 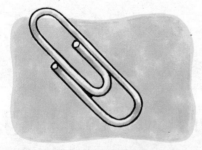  

● ▲ ■ Circle the object a magnet will attract.